What's In A DREAM?

If we study carefully the spirtual impressions left upon the dream mind, through the interpretations of this book, we will be able to shape our future in accordance with spiritual law.

The theory used in this book to interpret dreams is both simple and rational. By the using of it you will be surprised to find so many of the predictions fulfilled in your waking life. We deal with both the thought and the dream. The thought or sign implied in the object dreamed of and the influence surrounding it are always considered in the interpretation

date   thoughts

emotions

dream

feelings upon awakening

comments

A

Apples *

Ripe apples on a tree, means the time has arrived for you to realize your hopes; think over what you want to do, and go fearlessly ahead. Ripe on top of the tree, warns you not to aim too high. Apples on the ground imply that false friends, and flatterers are working you harm.

Actress. * To see in your dreams an actress, denotes that your present state will be one of unbroken pleasure and favor.

Acorns * .Seeing acorns in dreams, is portent of pleasant things ahead, and much gain is to be expected.

Afraid * To feel that you are afraid to proceed with some affair, or continue a journey, denotes that you will find trouble in your household, and enterprises will be unsuccessful.

Alabaster * To dream of alabaster, foretells success in marriage and all legitimate affairs. To break an alabaster figure or vessel, denotes sorrow and repentence

Alligator * To dream of an alligator, unless you kill it, is unfavorable to all persons connected with the dream. It is a dream of caution.

Age * To dream of age, portends failures in any kind of undertaking.

Anchor *.To dream of an anchor is favorable to sailors, if seas are calm. To others it portends separation from friends, change of residence, and foreign travel. Sweethearts are soon to quarrel if either sees an anchor.

date _____ thoughts _____

_____

_____

_____

emotions

_____

_____

dream

_____

_____

_____

_____

_____

_____

_____

feelings upon awakening

_____

_____

_____

comments

_____

POSITIVE OBSERVATION PROVES THE EXISTENCE OF A PSYCHIC WORLD, as real as the world known to our physical senses.

Because the soul acts at a distance by some power that belongs to it, are we authorized to conclude that it exists as something real, and that it is not the result of functions of the brain?

Does light really exist?
Does heat exist?
Does sound exist?
No.

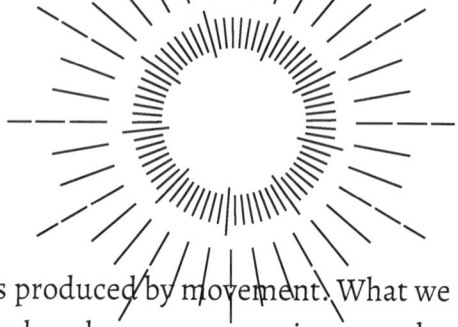

They are only manifestations produced by movement. What we call light is a sensation produced upon our optic nerve by the vibrations of ether, comprising between 400 and 756 trillions per second, undulations that are themselves very obscure.
What we call heat is a sensation produced by vibrations between 350 and 600 trillions.

The sun lights up space, as much at midnight as at midday. Its temperature is nearly 270 degrees below zero.

What we call sound is a sensation produced upon our auditory nerve by silent vibrations of the air, themselves comprising between
32,000 and 36,000 a second...

Very many scientific terms represent only results, not causes.

The soul may be in the same case.

date _____ thoughts _____

_____

_____

_____

emotions

_____

_____

_____

dream

_____

_____

_____

_____

_____

_____

_____

_____

feelings upon awakening

_____

_____

_____

comments

_____

_____

If you should pass on a train, at the speed of two miles a minute, through a forest of flowers and trees, your mind would be unable to distinguish one flower or tree from another.

It is in a similar way dream life and incidents may fall upon the mind.

A woman may dream of receiving a letter, and in the same connection see muddy water, or an arid landscape. Closely following, in waking life, she is astonished to receive a letter in about the same manner of her dream, but the muddy water and the arid landscape are missing.

This is a mixed dream and is due to more than one cause. The first part is literal in its fulfilment, and belongs to the spiritual class; the other part of the dream is subjective, and therefore allegorical in meaning.

Together with the letter, it was a forewarning of misfortune.These dreams are more difficult of interpretation than those belonging to the spiritual type. In such dreams you may see water, letters, houses, money, people, and countless other things. The next day you may cross water or receive a letter; the other things you may not see, but annoyance or pleasure will follow.

Again, you may have a similar dream and not receive a letter or cross water, but the waking life will be filled with the other dream pictures and you will experience disappointing or pleasant surprises as are indicated by the letter or water sign.

I have selected the allegorical type of dreams for the subject of this work. Dreams that are common occurrences and are thought by the world to be meaningless.I have endeavored, through the occult forces in and about me to find their esoteric or hidden import.

date   thoughts

_____

_____

_____

_____

                        emotions

_____

_____

                        dream

_____

_____

_____

_____

_____

_____

_____

                feelings upon awakening

_____

_____

                        comments

_____

Baby ~
To dream of crying babies, is indicative of ill health and disappointments.

Bacon
To dream of eating bacon is good, if some one is eating with you and hands are clean.

Bag-Pipe ~
This is not a bad dream, unless the music be harsh and the player in rags.

Bachelor ~
For a man to dream that he is a bachelor, is a warning for him to keep clear of women.

Buzzard ~
To dream that you hear a buzzard talking, foretells that some old scandal will arise and work you injury by your connection with it.

Banana ~
To dream of bananas, foretells that you will be mated to an uninteresting and an unloved companion.

Beans ~
This is a bad dream.
To see them growing, omens worries and sickness among children

Bear ~ significant of overwhelming competition in pursuits of every kind.

Brothel ~ To dream of being in a brothel, denotes you will encounter disgrace through your material indulgence.

Beauty ~ in any form is pre-eminently good

date   thoughts

emotions

dream

feelings upon awakening

comments

Dreams transpire on the subjective plane. They should therefore be interpreted by subjective intelligence.

This, I have honestly endeavored to do. Through the long hours of many nights

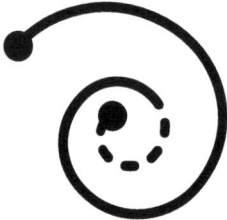

I have waited patiently and passively the automatic movement of my hand to write the subjective definitions without receiving a word or a single manifestation of intelligence, and again the mysterious forces would write as fast as my hand could move over the paper.

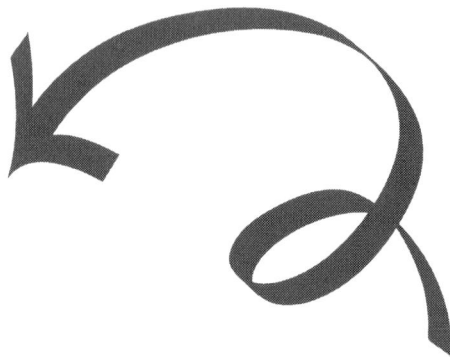

date   thoughts

_____

_____

_____

_____

emotions

_____

_____

dream

_____

_____

_____

_____

_____

_____

_____

feelings upon awakening

_____

_____

_____

comments

_____

I will leave it for my readers to draw their own conclusions as to whether automatic writing is the work of extraneous spirits, through the brain and intelligence of the medium, or the result of auto-suggestive influence upon the subjective personality.

It is argued by the Materialist, with some degree of strength, that the healthy man does not dream.

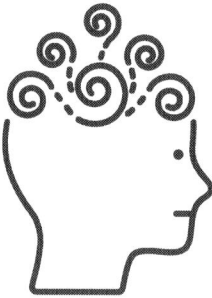

The personal self, in a normal state, cannot free itself from the past or from the anxieties of the future.

A wise doctor, in preparing medicine for a patient, considers well his age, temperament and his present condition. So should the interpreter of dreams ponder well the mental state, the health, habits and temperament of the dreamer. These things no one can know so well as the dreamer himself. He, therefore, with the aid of this book, will be able to interpret his dreams by the light that is in him.

date   thoughts

_____

_____

_____

_____

emotions

_____

_____

dream

_____

_____

_____

_____

_____

_____

_____

feelings upon awakening

_____

_____

_____

comments

_____

_____

Cabbage – It is bad to dream of cabbage. Disorders may run riot in all forms. To dream of seeing cabbage green, means unfaithfulness in love and infidelity in wedlock.

Canoe –
To paddle a canoe on a calm stream, denotes your perfect confidence in your own ability to conduct your business in a profitable way.

Chair –
To see a chair in your dream, denotes failure to meet some obligation.

Caterpillar –
To see a caterpillar in a dream, denotes that low and hypocritical people are in your immediate future, and you will do well to keep clear of deceitful appearances. You may suffer a loss in love or business.

Currying a Horse –
To dream of currying a horse, signifies that you will have a great many hard licks to make both with brain and hand before you attain to the heights of your ambition; but if you successfully curry him you will attain that height, whatever it may be.

Castle – To dream of being in a castle, you will be possessed of sufficient wealth to make life as you wish. You have prospects of being a great traveler, enjoying contact with people of many nations.

Candles – To see them burning with a clear and steady flame, denotes the constancy of those about you and a well-grounded fortune.

Counterfeit Money – To dream of counterfeit money, denotes you will have trouble with some unruly and worthless person. This dream always omens evil, whether you receive it or pass it.

date   thoughts
_____

_____

_____

_____

                                  emotions
_____

_____

                                  dream
_____

_____

_____

_____

_____

_____

_____

_____

                          feelings upon awakening
_____

_____

_____

                                  comments
_____

_____

HOW TO DEVELOP THE POWER TO DREAM

Keep the mind clear and as free from material rubbish as is possible and go to sleep in a negative condition (this will, of course, have to be cultivated by the subject).

A person can, if he will, completely relax his mind and body to the receptive mood required for dreams to appear as realities, or true explanations of future events.

* * * *

date   thoughts

emotions

dream

feelings upon awakening

comments

Devil =

To dream of the devil as being a large, imposingly dressed person, wearing many sparkling jewels on his body and hands, trying to persuade you to enter his abode, warns you that unscrupulous persons are seeking

your ruin by the most ingenious flattery. Young and innocent women, should seek the stronghold of friends after this dream, and avoid strange attentions, especially from married men. Women of low character, are likely to be robbed of jewels and money by seeming strangers.

Dance =

To see older people dancing, denotes a brighter outlook for business.To dream of dancing yourself, some unexpected good fortune will come to you.

Dandelions =

these blossoming in green foliage, foretells happy unions and prosperous surroundings.

Dice =

To dream of dice, is indicative of unfortunate speculations, and consequent misery and despair. It also foretells contagious sickness.

Donkey =

To dream of a donkey braying in your face, denotes that you are about to be publicly insulted by a lewd and unscrupulous person.

Door =

To dream of entering a door, denotes slander, and enemies from whom you are trying in vain to escape

Dragon =

To dream of a dragon, denotes that you allow yourself to be governed by your passions, and that you are likely to place yourself in the power of your enemies through those outbursts of sardonic tendencies. You should be warned by this dream to cultivate self-control.

date

thoughts

_____

emotions

_____

dream

_____

feelings upon awakening

_____

comments

The Bible, as well as other great books of historical and revealed religion, shows traces of a general and substantial belief in dreams.

Plato, Goethe, Shakespeare and Napoleon assigned to certain dreams prophetic value.

Joseph saw eleven stars of the Zodiac bow to himself, the twelfth star.

The famine of Egypt was revealed by a vision of fat and lean cattle.

The parents of Christ were warned of the cruel edict of Herod, and fled with the Divine Child into Egypt.

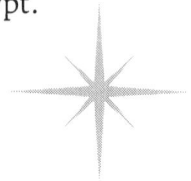

date   thoughts

_____

_____

_____

_____

emotions

_____

_____

dream

_____

_____

_____

_____

_____

_____

_____

feelings upon awakening

_____

_____

_____

comments

_____

The ultimatum of all human decrees and wisdom is to gratify the passions of the flesh at the expense of the spirit. The prophets and those who have stood nearest the fountain of universal knowledge used dreams with more frequency than any other mode of divination.

Profane, as well as sacred, history is threaded with incidents of dream prophecy. Ancient history relates that Gennadius was convinced of the immortality of his soul by conversing with an apparition in his dream.

Through the dream of Cecilia Metella, the wife of a Consul, the Roman Senate was induced to order the temple of Juno Sospita rebuilt.

The Emperor Marcian dreamed he saw the bow of the Hunnish conqueror break on the same night that Attila died.

Plutarch relates how Augustus, while ill, through the dream of a friend, was persuaded to leave his tent, which a few hours after was captured by the enemy, and the bed whereon he had lain was pierced with the enemies' swords.

If Julius Caesar had been less incredulous about dreams he would have listened to the warning which Calpurnia, his wife, received in a dream.

Croesus saw his son killed in a dream.

Petrarch saw his beloved Laura, in a dream, on the day she died, after which he wrote his beautiful poem, "The Triumph of Death."

date   thoughts

_____

_____

_____

_____

                        emotions

_____

_____

_____

                        dream

_____

_____

_____

_____

_____

_____

_____

_____

                feelings upon awakening

_____

_____

_____

                        comments

_____

To dream of

explosions

portends that disapproving actions of
those connected with you will cause
you transient displeasure and loss, and
that business will also displease you.
To think your face, or the face of
others, is blackened or mutilated,
signifies you will be accused of
indiscretion which will be unjust,
though circumstances may convict you.

To dream of an

eel

is good if you can
maintain your
grip on
him. Otherwise
fortune will be
fleeting.

To dream of

eyebrows,

denotes that you will
encounter sinister
obstacles in your
immediate future.

To see many

elephants,

denotes tremendous
prosperity. One alone
signifies you will live
in a small but solid
way.

To see an

eagle

soaring above you, denotes
lofty ambitions which you
will struggle fiercely to
realize, nevertheless you
will gain your desires.

date   thoughts

emotions

dream

feelings upon awakening

comments

Plato concurred in the general idea prevailing in his day, that there were divine manifestations to the soul in sleep.

Condorcet thought and wrote with greater fluency in his dreams than in waking life.

Coleridge, through dream influence, composed his "Kubla Khan."

The writers of Greek and Latin classics relate many instances of dream experiences. Homer accorded to some dreams divine origin.

During the third and fourth centuries, the supernatural origin of dreams was so generally accepted that the fathers, relying upon the classics and the Bible as authority, made this belief a doctrine of the Christian Church.

Synesius placed dreaming above all methods of divining the future; he thought it the surest, and open to the poor and rich alike.

Aristotle wrote: "There is a divination concerning some things in dreams not incredible."

Joan of Arc predicted her death.

date   thoughts

_____

_____

_____

_____

                        emotions

_____

_____

                        dream

_____

_____

_____

_____

_____

_____

_____

_____

                feelings upon awakening

_____

_____

_____

                        comments

_____

All these show unknown faculties in
the
~ Soul ~

Such at least is my own impression.

It seems to me that we cannot
reasonably attribute the prevision of
the future and mental sight to a
nervous action of the

~ brain ~

date   thoughts

_____

_____

_____

emotions

_____

_____

dream

_____

_____

_____

_____

_____

_____

_____

feelings upon awakening

_____

_____

comments

_____

We may see without eyes and hear without ears, not by unnatural excitement of our sense of vision or of hearing, for these accounts prove the contrary, but by some interior sense, psychic and mental.`

`THE SOUL, BY ITS INTERIOR VISION, MAY SEE NOT ONLY WHAT IS PASSING AT A GREAT DISTANCE, BUT IT MAY ALSO KNOW IN ADVANCE WHAT IS TO HAPPEN IN THE FUTURE. THE FUTURE EXISTS POTENTIALLY, DETERMINED BY CAUSES WHICH BRING TO PASS SUCCESSIVE EVENTS.

date   thoughts

emotions

dream

feelings upon awakening

comments

/Fairy /

To dream of a fairy, is a favorable omen to all classes, as it is always a scene with a beautiful face portrayed as a happy child, or woman.

/Fat/

To dream that you are getting fat, denotes that you are about to make a fortunate change in your life. To see others fat, signifies prosperity.

/Feet/

To dream of seeing your own feet, is omnious{sic} of despair. You will be overcome by the will and temper of another. To see others feet, denotes that you will maintain your rights in a pleasant, but determined way, and win for yourself a place above the common walks of life.

/Fingers/

To dream of seeing your fingers soiled or scratched, with the blood exuding, denotes much trouble and suffering. You will despair of making your way through life. To see beautiful hands, with white fingers, denotes that your love will be requited and that you will become renowned for your benevolence. To dream that your fingers are cut clean off, you will lose wealth and a legacy by the intervention of enemies.

/Feather/

To see chicken feathers, denotes small annoyances. To dream of buying or selling geese or duck feathers, denotes thrift and fortune.

/Fiend/

To dream that you encounter a fiend, forbodes reckless living and loose morals. For a woman, this dream signifies a blackened reputation.

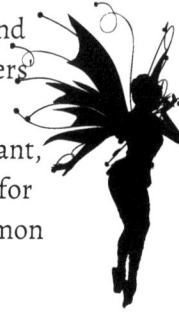

/Fish/

To dream that you see fish in clear-water streams, denotes that you will be favored by the rich and powerful.

F

date   thoughts

_____

_____

_____

_____

                        emotions

_____

_____

                        dream

_____

_____

_____

_____

_____

_____

_____

                feelings upon awakening

_____

_____

_____

                        comments

_____

These phenomena prove, I think, that the soul exists, and that it is endowed with faculties at present unknown. That is the logical way of commencing our study, which in the end may lead us to the problem of the after-life and immortality.

A thought can be transmitted to the mind of another.

There are mental transmissions, communications of thoughts, and psychic currents between human souls. Space appears to be no obstacle in these cases, and time sometimes seems to be annihilated.[11]

date   thoughts

emotions

dream

feelings upon awakening

comments

MAN CANNOT CONTRADICT THE LAWS OF NATURE. BUT, ARE ALL THE LAWS OF NATURE YET UNDERSTOOD?

Real philosophy seeks rather to solve than to deny.

date   thoughts

_____

_____

_____

                                  emotions

_____

_____

                                  dream

_____

_____

_____

_____

_____

_____

_____

                        feelings upon awakening

_____

_____

_____

                                  comments

_____

_____

Garden

To see a garden in your dreams, filled with evergreen and flowers, denotes great peace of mind and comfort.

Goat.

To dream of goats wandering around a farm, is significant of seasonable weather and a fine yield of crops. To see them otherwise, denotes cautious dealings and a steady increase of wealth.

Grasshopper

To dream of seeing grasshoppers on green vegetables, denotes that enemies threaten your best interests.

Gypsy

For a woman to have a gypsy tell her fortune, an omen of a speedy and unwise marriage. If she is already married, she will be unduly jealous of her husband. For a man to hold any conversation with a gypsy, he will be likely to lose valuable property.

Garlic

To dream of passing through a garlic patch, denotes a rise from penury to prominence and wealth. To a young woman this denotes that she will marry from a sense of business, and love will not be considered.

Garter

For a married man to dream of a garter, foretells that his wife will hear of his clandestine attachments, and he will have a stormy scene.

date   thoughts

_____

_____

_____

emotions

_____

_____

dream

_____

_____

_____

_____

_____

_____

feelings upon awakening

_____

_____

comments

_____

Nature is three-fold, so is man;
male and female, son or soul.
The union of one and two
produce the triad or the trinity
which underlies the philosophy
of the ancients.

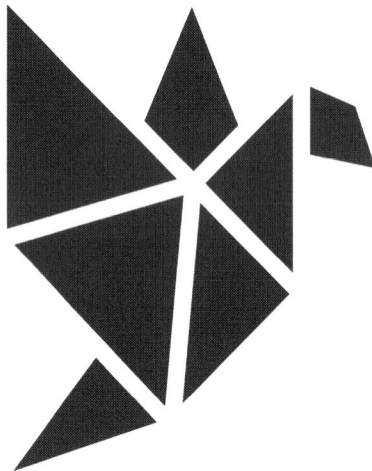

date   thoughts

_____

_____

_____

_____

                        emotions

_____

_____

                        dream

_____

_____

_____

_____

_____

_____

_____

_____

                feelings upon awakening

_____

_____

_____

                        comments

_____

_____

The soul is not only the son or creation of man, but it is the real man. It is the inner imperishable double or imprint of what has outwardly and inwardly transpired. All thoughts, desires and actions enter the soul through the objective mind.

date   thoughts

_____

_____

_____

emotions

_____

_____

dream

_____

_____

_____

_____

_____

_____

_____

feelings upon awakening

_____

_____

_____

comments

_____

Hammer: To dream of seeing a hammer, denotes you will have some discouraging obstacles to overcome in order to establish firmly your fortune.

Harlequin: If you dream of a harlequin, trouble will beset you. To be dressed as a harlequin, denotes passionate error and unwise attacks on strength and purse. Designing women will lure you to paths of sin.

Hen: To dream of hens, denotes pleasant family reunions with added members.

Hook: To dream of a hook, foretells unhappy obligations will be assumed by you.

Honeysuckle: To see or gather, honeysuckles, denotes that you will be contentedly prosperous and your marriage will be a singularly happy one.

Horse: To dream of horses, you will amass wealth and enjoy life to its fullest extent.

Hat.

If you lose your hat, you may expect unsatisfactory business and failure of persons to keep important engagements. For a man to dream that he wears a new hat, predicts change of place and business, which will be very much to his advantage. For a woman to dream that she wears a fine new hat, denotes the attainment of wealth, and she will be the object of much admiration. For the wind to blow your hat off, denotes sudden changes in affairs, and somewhat for the worse.

date   thoughts

_____

_____

_____

_____

                              emotions

_____

_____

_____

                               dream

_____

_____

_____

_____

_____

_____

_____

_____

                    feelings upon awakening

_____

_____

_____

                             comments

_____

_____

Man has also a spiritual body, subjective to, and more ethereal than the soul. It is an infinitesimal atom, and is related in substance to the spiritual or infinite mind of the universe. Just as the great physical sun, the center of visible light, life and heat, is striving to purify the foul miasma of the marsh and send its luminous messages of love into the dark crevices of the earth, so the Great Spiritual Sun, of which the former is a visible prototype or reflection, is striving to illuminate with Divine Wisdom the personal soul and mind of man, thus enabling him to become cognizant of the spiritual or Christ presence within.

date   thoughts

_____

_____

_____

_____

                        emotions

_____

_____

                        dream

_____

_____

_____

_____

_____

_____

_____

_____

                feelings upon awakening

_____

_____

_____

                        comments

_____

_____

The objective mind is most active when the body is awake. The subjective influences are most active, and often fill the mind with impressions, while the physical body is asleep. The spiritual intelligence can only intrude itself when the human will is suspended, or passive to external states. A man who lives only on the sensual plane will receive his knowledge through the senses, and will not, while in that state, receive spiritual impressions or warning dreams.

date   thoughts

emotions

dream

feelings upon awakening

comments

Ink>

To see ink spilled over one's clothing, many small and spiteful meannesses will be wrought you through envy.young woman sees.To dream that you have ink on your fingers, you will be jealous and seek to injure some one unless you exercise your better nature.

Indigo>

To see indigo in a dream, denotes you will deceive friendly persons in order to cheat them out of their be longings. To see indigo water, foretells you will be involved in an ugly love affair.

Ironing>

To dream of ironing, denotes domestic comforts and orderly business.

Island>

To dream that you are on an island in a clear stream, signifies pleasant journeys and fortunate enterprises.

Ivy>

To dream of ivy growing on trees or houses, predicts excellent health and increase of fortune. Innumerable joys will succeed this dream. To a young woman, it augurs many prized distinctions. If she sees ivy clinging to the wall in the moonlight, she will have clandestine meetings with young men.Withered ivy, denotes broken engagements and sadness.

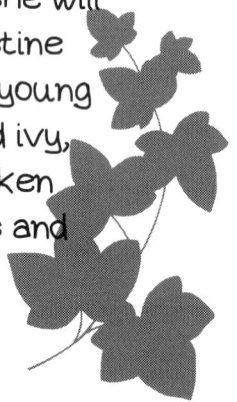

I

date   thoughts

emotions

dream

feelings upon awakening

comments

David, while intoxicated with the wine of love, from languishing in the seductive embrace of the beautiful bathing nymph, Bathsheba, heard the voice of Nathan.

Surely God is no respecter of persons, and will speak to all classes if the people will not stiffen their necks or harden their hearts.

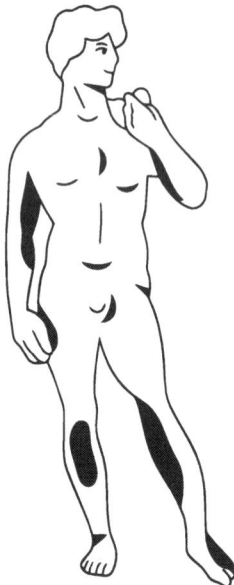

date   thoughts

emotions

dream

feelings upon awakening

comments

Women dream more often and more vividly than men, because their dream composition is influenced and allied to external environments.

date

thoughts

emotions

dream

feelings upon awakening

comments

[Javelin] To dream of defending yourself with a javelin, your most private affairs will be searched into to establish claims of dishonesty, and you will prove your innocence after much wrangling.

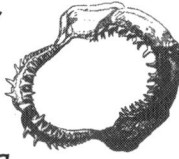

[Jaws] If your own jaws ache with pain, you will be exposed to climatic changes, and malaria may cause you loss in health and finances.

[Jester] To dream of a jester, foretells you will ignore important things in looking after silly affairs.

[Jewels] To wear them, brings rank and satisfied ambitions. To see others wearing them, distinguished places will be held by you, or by some friend.

[Jig] To dance a jig, denotes cheerful occupations and light pleasures.

[Jug] If you drink wine from a jug, you will enjoy robust health and find pleasure in all circles. Optimistic views will possess you.

date _____ thoughts _____

_____

_____

_____

emotions

_____

_____

dream

_____

_____

_____

_____

_____

_____

_____

feelings upon awakening

_____

_____

_____

comments

_____

_____

All dreams possess an element of warning or prescience; some more than others. This is unknown to the many, but is known to the observing few. There are many people who have no natural taste for music, and who do not know one note from another. There are also those who cannot distinguish one color from another. To the former there is no harmony of sound, and to the latter there is no blending of colors.

date   thoughts
_____

_____

_____

_____

                                  emotions
_____

_____

                                  dream
_____

_____

_____

_____

_____

_____

_____

                        feelings upon awakening
_____

_____

                                  comments
_____

_____

To see a kangaroo in your dreams, you will outwit a wily enemy who seeks to place you in an unfavorable position before the public and the person you are striving to win.

To dream of keys, denotes unexpected changes.

To dream of hearing katydids, is a prognostic of misfortune and unusual dependence on others. If any sick person ask you what they are, foretells there will be surprising events in your present and future.

For a woman to dream of a beautiful fat, white kitten, omens artful deception will be practised upon her, which will almost ensnare her to destruction, but her good sense and judgment will prevail in warding off unfortunate complications. If the kittens are soiled, or colored and lean, she will be victimized into glaring indiscretions.

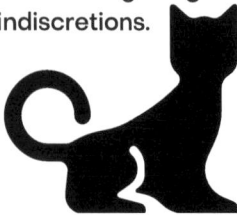

A Kaleidoscope working before you in a dream portends swift changes with little of favorable promise in them.

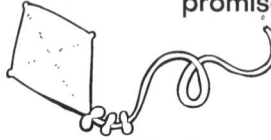

To dream of flying a kite, denotes a great show of wealth, or business, but with little true soundness to it all.

To see Krishna in your dreams, denotes that your greatest joy will be in pursuit of occult knowledge, and you will school yourself to the taunts of friends, and cultivate a philosophical bearing toward life and sorrow.

To dream that your knees are too large, denotes sudden ill luck for you.If they are stiff and pain you, swift and fearful calamity awaits you.

date _____ thoughts _____

_____

_____

_____

emotions

_____

_____

dream

_____

_____

_____

_____

_____

_____

_____

feelings upon awakening

_____

_____

_____

comments

_____

A man dreams of walking through green fields of corn, grass or wheat.

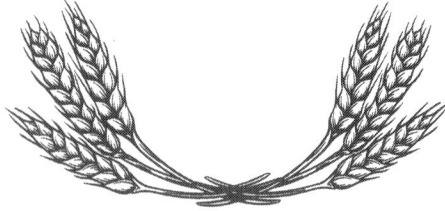

He notes after such dreams prosperous conditions follow for at least a few days.

He also notes, if the area over which he passes is interspersed with rocks or other adverse signs, good and bad follow in the wake of the dream.

If he succeeds in climbing a mountain and finds the top barren he will accomplish his object, but the deal will prove unprofitable.

If it is green and spring-like in appearance, it will yield good results.

If he sees muddy water, sickness, business depression or causes for jealousy may develop

date _____ thoughts _____

_____

_____

_____

emotions

_____

_____

dream

_____

_____

_____

_____

_____

_____

_____

feelings upon awakening

_____

_____

comments

_____

A nightmare suggests to the dreamer to be careful of health and diet, to relax his whole body, to sleep with his arms down and keep plenty of fresh air in the room.

date

thoughts

emotions

dream

feelings upon awakening

comments

There are three pure types of dreams, namely, subjective, physical and spiritual.

They relate to the past, present and future, and are influenced by past or subjective, physical and spiritual causes.

The latter is always deeply prophetic, especially when it leaves a vivid impression on the conscious mind.

The former, too, possesses an element of warning and prophecy, though the true meaning is hidden in symbols or allegory.

They are due to contingent mental pictures of the past falling upon the conscious mind of the dreamer.

Thus he is back at the old home, and finds mother pale and aged, or ruddy and healthy, and the lawn withered or green. It all augurs, according to the aspect the picture assumes, ill or good fortune.

date   thoughts

_____

_____

_____

_____

                                 emotions

_____

_____

_____

                                  dream

_____

_____

_____

_____

_____

_____

_____

_____

                      feelings upon awakening

_____

_____

_____

                                 comments

_____

Legerdemain# To dream of practising legerdemain, or seeing others doing so, signifies you will be placed in a position where your energy and power of planning will be called into strenuous play to extricate yourself.

L

Lemons# To dream of seeing lemons on their native trees among rich foliage, denotes jealousy toward some beloved object, but demonstrations will convince you of the absurdity of the charge. To eat lemons, foretells humiliation and disappointments.

Lizard# To dream of lizards, foretells attacks upon you by enemies.

Leopard# To dream of a leopard attacking you, denotes that while the future seemingly promises fair, success holds many difficulties through misplaced confidence.

Lobster# To dream of seeing lobsters, denotes great favors, and riches will endow you.

Lion# To dream of a lion, signifies that a great force is driving you.

Lightning# Lightning in your dreams, foreshadows happiness and prosperity of short duration.

date   thoughts

_____

_____

_____

_____

                              emotions

_____

_____

                              dream

_____

_____

_____

_____

_____

_____

_____

_____

                      feelings upon awakening

_____

_____

_____

                              comments

_____

Dreams induced by opiates, fevers, mesmerism and ill health come under the class of physical dreams which are more or less unimportant.

They are usually superinduced by the anxious waking mind, and when this is so they possess no prophetic significance.

A man who gambles is liable to dream of cards; if he dreams of them in deep sleep the warning is to be heeded; but if it comes as a reverie while he sleeps lightly he should regard it as worthless. Such dreams reflect only the present condition of the body and mind of the dreamer; but as the past and present enter into shaping the future, the reflections thus left on the waking mind should not go by unheeded.

date   thoughts

_____

_____

_____

_____

emotions

_____

_____

dream

_____

_____

_____

_____

_____

_____

_____

feelings upon awakening

_____

_____

_____

comments

_____

Morocco... To see morocco in your dreams, foretells that you will receive substantial aid from unexpected sources. Your love will be rewarded by faithfulness.

Monkey... To dream of a monkey, denotes that deceitful people will flatter you to advance their own interests.

Magpie... To dream of a magpie, denotes much dissatisfation and quarrels.The dreamer should guard well his conduct and speech after this dream.

Milk... To dream of drinking milk, denotes abundant harvest to the farmer and pleasure in the home; for a traveler, it foretells a fortunate voyage. This is a very propitious dream for women.To see milk in large quantities, signifies riches and health.

Mocking-bird... To see or hear a mocking-bird, signifies you will be invited to go on a pleasant visit to friends, and your affairs will move along smoothly and prosperously. For a woman to see a wounded or dead one, her disagreement with a friend or lover is signified.

Mice... To dream of mice, foretells domestic troubles and the insincerity of friends.

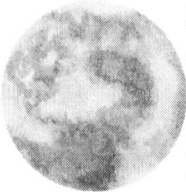

Moon... For a young woman to dream that she appeals to the moon to know her fate, denotes that she will soon be rewarded with marriage to the one of her choice. If she sees two moons, she will lose her lover by being mercenary. If she sees the moon grow dim, she will let the supreme happiness of her life slip for want of womanly tact.

date   thoughts

emotions

dream

feelings upon awakening

comments

We often observe matters of dress and exterior appearance through mirrors, and we soon make the necessary alterations to put our bodies in harmony with existing formalities.

Then, why not study more seriously the mental images reflected from the mirror of the soul upon our minds through the occult processes within us?

date

thoughts

_____

_____

_____

emotions

_____

_____

dream

_____

_____

_____

_____

_____

_____

_____

feelings upon awakening

_____

_____

comments

_____

Thirdly, the spiritual dreams are brought about by the higher self penetrating the soul realm, and reflecting upon the waking mind approaching events. When we put our animal mind and soul in harmony with our higher self we become one with it, and, therefore, one with the universal mind or will by becoming a part of it. It is through the higher self we reach the infinite. It is through the lower self we fall into the whirlpool of matter.

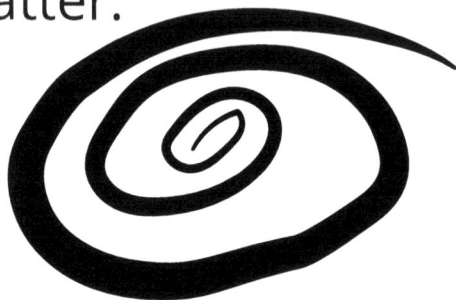

date _____ thoughts _____

_____

_____

_____

emotions

_____

_____

dream

_____

_____

_____

_____

_____

_____

_____

feelings upon awakening

_____

_____

comments

_____

(Nightmare) To dream of being attacked with this hideous sensation, denotes wrangling and failure in business.

For a young woman, this is a dream prophetic of disappointment and unmerited slights. It may also warn the dreamer to be careful of her health, and food.

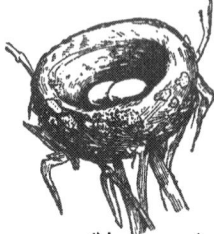

(Needle) To use a needle in your dream, is a warning of approaching affliction, in which you will suffer keenly the loss of sympathy, which is rightfully yours. To dream of threading a needle, denotes that you will be burdened with the care of others than your own household.

(Necklace) For a woman to dream of receiving a necklace, omens for her a loving husband and a beautiful home. To lose a necklace, she will early feel the heavy hand of bereavement.

N

(Nest) To dream of seeing birds' nests, denotes that you will be interested in an enterprise which will be prosperous. For a young woman, this dream foretells change of abode.

(Necromancer) To dream of a necromancer and his arts, denotes that you are threatened with strange acquaintances who will influence you for evil.

(Neck) To dream that you see your own neck, foretells that vexatious family relations will interfere with your business. To admire the neck of another, signifies your worldly mindedness will cause broken domestic ties.

(Nymph) To see nymphs bathing in clear water, denotes that passionate desires will find an ecstatic realization. Convivial entertainments will enchant you.

(Nose) To see your own nose, indicates force of character, and consciousness of your ability to accomplish whatever enterprise you may choose to undertake.

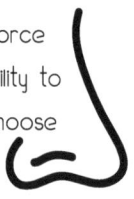

date _____ thoughts _____

_____

_____

_____

emotions

_____

_____

dream

_____

_____

_____

_____

_____

_____

_____

_____

feelings upon awakening

_____

_____

_____

comments

_____

Dreams are a part of the universal mind until they transpire in the life of man.

After this they go to make a part of the personal soul. Whatever has not taken place in the mind, or life of man, belongs exclusively to the impersonal mind.

But as soon as a man lives or sees a thing, that thing instantly becomes a part of his soul; hence, the clairvoyant, or mind reader, never perceives beyond the personal ego, as the future belongs exclusively to God or the universal mind, and has no material, subjective existence; therefore, it cannot be known except through the channels of the higher self, which is the Truth or the Word that is constantly striving to manifest itself through the flesh.

date   thoughts

_____

_____

_____

emotions

_____

_____

dream

_____

_____

_____

_____

_____

_____

_____

feelings upon awakening

_____

_____

comments

_____

_____

Our psychical research people give us conclusive proof of mental telepathy or telegraphy between finite minds. Thus communications or impressions are conveyed many miles from one mind to another. This phenomenon is easier when one or both of the subjects are in a state of somnambulence or asleep.

date   thoughts

_____

_____

_____

                                    emotions

_____

_____

                                    dream

_____

_____

_____

_____

_____

_____

_____

_____

                        feelings upon awakening

_____

_____

                                    comments

_____

In thought transference or mind reading

it is absolutely necessary to have a positive and a negative subject. Through the same law that mental impressions are telegraphed from one finite mind to another a man may place himself in harmony with the infinite mind and thus receive true and healthful warnings of coming evil or good. Homer, Aristotle and other writers of the ancient classics thought this not improbable.

date   thoughts

_____

_____

_____

_____

emotions

_____

_____

dream

_____

_____

_____

_____

_____

_____

_____

_____

feelings upon awakening

_____

_____

_____

comments

_____

_____

To dream of handling **+OARS+** portends disappointments for you, inasmuch as you will sacrifice your own pleasure for the comfort of others.To lose an oar, denotes vain efforts to carry out designs satisfactorily.

Seeing quantities of **+onions+** in your dreams, represents the amount of spite and envy that you will meet, by being successful.If you eat them, you will overcome all opposition.

An **+obelisk+** looming up stately and cold in your dreams is the forerunner of melancholy tidings.For lovers to stand at the base of an obelisk, denotes fatal disagreements.

If you wear **+ornaments+** in dreams, you will have a flattering honor conferred upon you.

To dream of consulting an **+oculist+** denotes that you will be dissatisfied with your progress in life, and will use artificial means of advancement.

Gathering **+olives+** with a merry band of friends, foretells favorable results in business, and delightful surprises.If you take them from bottles, it foretells conviviality

To dream of an **+ostrich+** denotes that you will secretly amass wealth, but at the same time maintain degrading intrigues with women.

date   thoughts

_____

_____

_____

emotions

_____

_____

dream

_____

_____

_____

_____

_____

_____

_____

feelings upon awakening

_____

_____

comments

_____

In sleep we see, without being awakened, the angry lightning rend the midnight clouds, and hear the explosive thunder hurl its fury at us; but can we explain it any more than our scientist can explain the natural forces of thought, of love and hate, or the subtle intuition of woman?

date   thoughts

_____

_____

_____

_____

                        emotions

_____

_____

                        dream

_____

_____

_____

_____

_____

_____

_____

_____

                feelings upon awakening

_____

_____

_____

                        comments

_____

The reader should ever keep before his mind the fact that no man ever had the same dream twice. He may have had very similar dreams, but some detail will be missing. Nature seems to abhor duplicates. You could no more find two dreams alike than you could find facsimiles in two blades of grass. A man cannot live two days exactly alike. Different influences and passions will possess him. Consequently, no two dreams can be had under exactly the same influences. Stereotypes are peculiarly the invention of man and not of God or nature.

date   thoughts

emotions

dream

feelings upon awakening

comments

Pyramid ~ To dream of pyramids, denotes that many changes will come to you.

Porpoise. To see a porpoise in your dreams, denotes enemies are thrusting your interest aside, through your own inability to keep people interested in you.

Porcupine ~ For a young woman to dream of a porcupine, portends that she will fear her lover.

Peacock ~ For persons dreaming of peacocks, there lies below the brilliant and flashing ebb and flow of the stream of pleasure and riches, the slums of sorrow and failure, which threaten to mix with its clearness at the least disturbing influence.

Pagoda ~ To see a pagoda in your dreams, denotes that you will soon go on a long desired journey.

Palm Tree ~ Palm trees seen in your dreams, are messages of hopeful situations and happiness of a high order.

Parrot ~ Parrots chattering in your dreams, signifies frivolous employments and idle gossip among your friends.

Pier ~ To stand upon a pier in your dream, denotes that you will be brave in your battle for recognition in prosperity's realm, and that you will be admitted to the highest posts of honor. If you strive to reach a pier and fail, you will lose the distinction you most coveted.

Pickles ~ To dream of pickles, denotes that you will follow worthless pursuits if you fail to call energy and judgment to your aid.

Passenger ~ To dream that you see passengers coming in with their luggage, denotes improvement in your surroundings.

date   thoughts

emotions

dream

feelings upon awakening

comments

Since it is impossible to find a man twice in exactly the same mental state, it is equally impossible for him to dream the same dream twice

So with dream symbols. We may know they are fraught with evil or good, as in the case of Pilate's wife, but we cannot tell their full meaning until their reflections materialize before the objective sense.

date   thoughts

_____

_____

_____

_____

                        emotions

_____

_____

_____

                        dream

_____

_____

_____

_____

_____

_____

_____

_____

                feelings upon awakening

_____

_____

_____

                        comments

_____

_____

The mind loses its reason or will in sleep, but a supersensitive perception is awakened, and, as it regains consciousness from sleep, the sound of a knock on the wall may be magnified into a pistol shot.

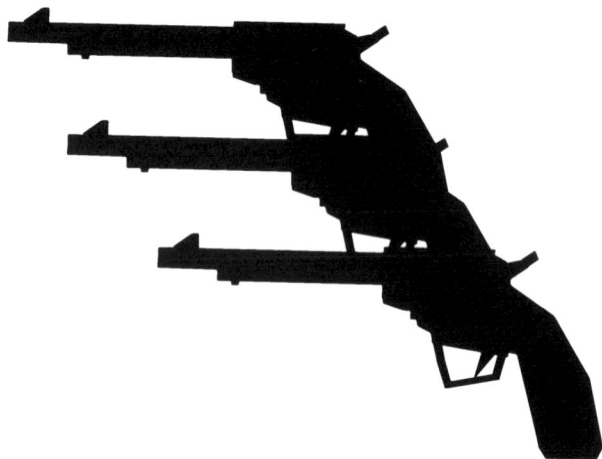

date   thoughts

_____

_____

_____

emotions

_____

_____

dream

_____

_____

_____

_____

_____

_____

_____

feelings upon awakening

_____

_____

_____

comments

_____

The sleeping mind is not only supersensitive as to existing external sounds and light, but it frequently sees hours and days ahead of the waking mind.

date

thoughts

_____

_____

_____

emotions

_____

_____

dream

_____

_____

_____

_____

_____

_____

_____

feelings upon awakening

_____

_____

comments

_____

"Queen"

To dream of a queen, foretells succesful ventures. If she looks old or haggard, there will be disappointments connected with your pleasures.

"Quail"

To see quails in your dream, is a very favorable omen, if they are alive; if dead, you will undergo serious ill luck.To shoot quail, foretells that ill feelings will be shown by you to your best friends.

"Quarry"

To dream of being in a quarry and seeing the workmen busy, denotes that you will advance by hard labor.

"Quicksand"

To find yourself in quicksand while dreaming, you will meet with loss and deceit.If you are unable to overcome it, you will be involved in overwhelming misfortunes.

"Quagmire"

To dream of being in a quagmire, implies your inability to meet obligations. To see others thus situated, denotes that the failures of others will be felt by you. Illness is sometimes indicated by this dream

"Question"

To ask a question, foretells that you will earnestly strive for truth and be successful.If you are questioned, you will be unfairly dealt with.

"Quills"

To dream of quills, denotes to the literary inclined a season of success.

"Quilts"

If the quilts are clean, but having holes in them, she will win a husband who appreciates her worth, but he will not be the one most desired by her for a companion. If the quilts are soiled, she will bear evidence of carelessness in her dress and manners, and thus fail to secure a very upright husband.

date   thoughts

_____

_____

_____

_____

                                  emotions

_____

_____

_____

                                   dream

_____

_____

_____

_____

_____

_____

_____

_____

                     feelings upon awakening

_____

_____

_____

                                  comments

_____

_____

So in sleep, man dreams the future by intuitive perception of invisible signs or influences, while awake he reasons it out by cause and effect. The former seems to be the law of the spiritual world, while the latter would appear to be the law of the material world. Man should not depend alone upon either. Together they proclaim the male and female principle of existence and should find harmonious consummation.

date   thoughts

_____

_____

_____

                        emotions

_____

_____

                        dream

_____

_____

_____

_____

_____

_____

_____

                feelings upon awakening

_____

_____

_____

                        comments

_____

_____

In this manner only can man hope to achieve that perfect normal state to which the best thought of the human race is aspiring, where he can create and control influences instead of being created and controlled by them, as the majority of us are at the present day.

date   thoughts

emotions

dream

feelings upon awakening

comments

Rabbit:: To dream of rabbits, foretells favorable turns in conditions, and you will be more pleased with your gains than formerly.

Rosemary:: If seen in dreams, denotes that sadness and indifference will cause unhappiness in homes where there is every appearance of prosperity.

Rain:: To be out in a clear shower of rain, denotes that pleasure will be enjoyed with the zest of youth, and prosperity will come to you.If the rain descends from murky clouds, you will feel alarmed over the graveness of your undertakings.

Raspberry:: To see raspberries in a dream, foretells you are in danger of entanglements which will prove interesting before you escape from them.

Rat:: To dream of rats, denotes that you will be deceived, and injured by your neighbors. Quarrels with your companions is also foreboded.

Ribbon:: To dream of long, flowing ribbon denotes practical cares will not trouble you greatly.

Reading:: To be engaged in reading in your dreams, denotes that you will excel in some work, which appears difficult.

Rum:: To dream of drinking rum, foretells that you will have wealth, but will lack moral refinement, as you will lean to gross pleasures.

Reindeer:: To dream of a reindeer, signifies faithful discharge of duties, and remaining staunch to friends in their adversity.To drive them, foretells that you will have hours of bitter anguish, but friends will attend you.

date   thoughts
_____

_____

_____

_____

                        emotions
_____

_____

_____

                        dream
_____

_____

_____

_____

_____

_____

_____

_____

                feelings upon awakening
_____

_____

_____

                        comments
_____

_____

God, the highest subjective source of intelligence, may in a dream leave impressions or presentiments on the mind of man, the highest objective source of intelligence.

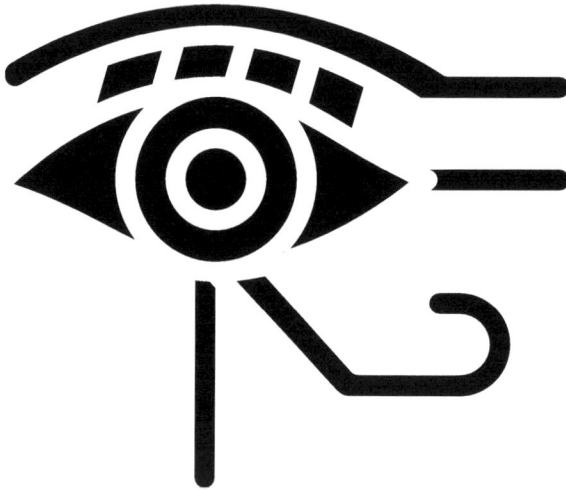

The physical sun sends its light into the dark corners of the earth, and God, the Spiritual Sun, imparts spiritual light into the passive and receptive soul.

date   thoughts

_____

_____

_____

                              emotions

_____

_____

                              dream

_____

_____

_____

_____

_____

_____

_____

                    feelings upon awakening

_____

_____

_____

                              comments

_____

_____

The dream mind is often influenced by the waking mind. When the waking mind dwells upon any subject, the dream mind is more or less influenced by it, and it often assists the waking mind in solving difficult problems. The personal future, embodied in the active states of the universal mind, may affect the dream mind, producing premonitions of death, accidents and misfortune.

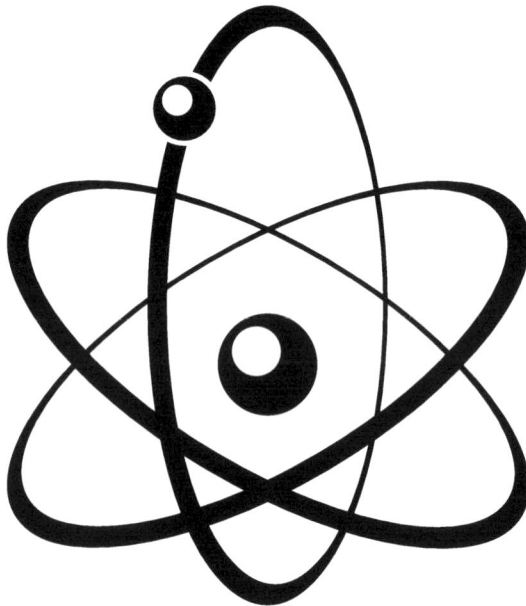

date   thoughts

_____

_____

_____

                                  emotions

_____

_____

                                  dream

_____

_____

_____

_____

_____

_____

_____

                          feelings upon awakening

_____

_____

                                  comments

_____

Sea Foam | For a woman to dream of sea foam foretells that indiscriminate and demoralizing pleasures will distract her from the paths of rectitude. If she wears a bridal veil of sea foam, she will engulf herself in material pleasure to the exclusion of true refinement and innate modesty. She will be likely to cause sorrow to some of those dear to her, through their inability to gratify her ambition.

Seaport | To dream of visiting a seaport, denotes that you will have opportunities of traveling and acquiring knowledge, but there will be some who will object to your anticipated tours.

Shells | To walk among and gather shells in your dream, denotes extravagance. Pleasure will leave you naught but exasperating regrets and memories.

Shakspeare | To dream of Shakspeare, denotes that unhappiness and dispondency will work much anxiety to momentous affairs, and love will be stripped of passion's fever.

Seducer | For a young woman to dream of being seduced, foretells that she will be easily influenced by showy persons.

Sun | To see the sunset, is prognostic of joys and wealth passing their zenith, and warns you to care for your interests with renewed vigilance.

Swan | Seeing white swans floating on placid waters, foretells prosperous outlooks and delightful experiences.

date   thoughts
_____

_____

_____

_____

                                  emotions
_____

_____

                                  dream
_____

_____

_____

_____

_____

_____

_____

_____

_____

                          feelings upon awakening
_____

_____

_____

                                  comments
_____

_____

The objective mind rejoices or laments over the aspects of the past and present, while the spiritual mind, striving with the personal future, either laments or rejoices over the prospective conditions.

One is the barometer of the past, while the other is the barometer of the future.

date   thoughts

_____

_____

_____

_____

                              emotions

_____

_____

                               dream

_____

_____

_____

_____

_____

_____

_____

_____

                      feelings upon awakening

_____

_____

_____

                              comments

_____

Thoughts proceed from the visible mind and dreams from the invisible mind.

The average waking mind receives and retains only a few of the lessons of life. It is largely filled with idle and incoherent thoughts that are soon forgotten.

The same may be truly said of the dream mind. Many of our day thoughts are day dreams, just as many of our night dreams are night thoughts. Our day deeds of evil or good pierce or soothe the conscience, just as our night symbols of sorrow and joy sadden or please the objective senses.

Our day's thoughts are filled with the warnings and presence of the inner mind and our night's thoughts are tinctured and often controlled by our external mind.

date
thoughts

emotions

dream

feelings upon awakening

comments

Tadpole. To dream of tadpoles, foretells uncertain speculation will bring cause for uneasiness in business. For a young woman to see them in clear water, foretells she will form a relation with a wealthy but immoral man.

Trousers. If you put them on wrong side out, you will find that a fascination is fastening its hold upon you.

Talisman. To dream that you wear a talisman, implies you will have pleasant companions and enjoy favors from the rich. For a young woman to dream her lover gives her one, denotes she will obtain her wishes concerning marriage.

Tambourine. To dream of a tambourine, signifies you will have enjoyment in some unusual event which will soon take place.

Tarantula. To see a tarantula in your dream, signifies enemies are about to overwhelm you with loss. To kill one, denotes you will be successful after much ill-luck.

Thorns. To dream of thorns, is an omen of dissatisfaction, and evil will surround every effort to advancement.If the thorns are hidden beneath green foliage, you prosperity will be interfered with by secret enemies.

Tiger.　To see one running away from you, is a sign that you will overcome opposition, and rise to high positions.To see them in cages, foretells that you will foil your adversaries.

Thimble. If you use a thimble in your dreams, you will have many others to please besides yourself. If a woman, you will have your own position to make.

Toad.　If a woman, your good name is threatened with scandal.To kill a toad, foretells that your judgment will be harshly criticised.

date   thoughts

_____

_____

_____

_____

emotions

_____

_____

dream

_____

_____

_____

_____

_____

_____

_____

feelings upon awakening

_____

_____

comments

_____

Everything that exists upon earth has its ethereal counterpart.

Christ said: As a man thinketh so is he.

A Hindu proverb says: Man is a creature of reflection; he becomes that upon which he reflects.

A modern metaphysicist says: Our thoughts are real substance and leave their images upon our personality, they fill our aura with beauty or ugliness according to our intents and purposes in life. Each evil thought or action has its pursuing phantom, each smile or kindly deed its guiding angel, we leave wherever we ignobly stand, a tomb and an epitaph to haunt us through the furnace of conscience and memory.

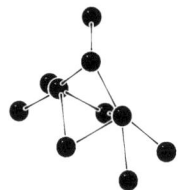

date   thoughts

emotions

dream

feelings upon awakening

comments

U

United States Mail Box

To see a United States mail box, in a dream, denotes that you are about to enter into transactions which will be claimed to be illegal.

Urn

To dream of an urn, foretells you will prosper in some respects, and in others disfavor will be apparent. To see broken urns, unhappiness will confront you.

Uniform

To see a uniform in your dream, denotes that you will have influential friends to aid you in obtaining your desires.

Usurper

To dream that you are a usurper, foretells you will have trouble in establishing a good title to property. If others are trying to usurp your rights, there will be a struggle between you and your competitors, but you will eventually win. For a young woman to have this dream, she will be a party to a spicy rivalry, in which she will win.

Umbrella

To dream of carrying an umbrella, denotes that trouble and annoyances will beset you. To see others carrying them, foretells that you will be appealed to for aid by charity.

date   thoughts

_____

_____

_____

_____

                        emotions

_____

_____

                        dream

_____

_____

_____

_____

_____

_____

_____

_____

_____

_____

            feelings upon awakening

_____

_____

_____

                        comments

_____

_____

WE MUST THEREFORE LOOK TO OTHER SOURCES FOR AN EXPLANATION.

Was it the higher self that manifested to Abraham in the dim ages of the world? Was it the Divine Voice that gave solace to Krishna in his abstraction? Was it the unerring light that preceded Gautama into the strange solitudes of Asia? Was it the small voice that Elijah heard in the desert of Shurr? Was it the Comforter of Jesus in the wilderness and the garden of distress? Or, was it Paul's indwelling spirit of this earthly tabernacle?

date   thoughts

_____

_____

_____

_____

emotions

_____

_____

dream

_____

_____

_____

_____

_____

_____

_____

feelings upon awakening

_____

_____

_____

comments

_____

FRAGMENTARY THOUGHTS FROM DREAM REALMS:

Man is a little circle or world composed of the infinitesimal atoms thrown off from the great circle he catches more material he increases his circle to objective or subjective growth: if he absorbs great circle according to the assimilation of the food he receives from the parent. It is optional or spiritual or mind atoms as they fall from the material manna as it is disseminated of supply to some of the smallest results should be avoided in computing the length and breadth of the compound into a perfect circle of man's physical and mental world, than is the exterior life. Objective life is the exterior life of man. The mind receives education from communing with the dream life. Dream life is fuller of meaning and teaching, together with a tender care of other parts, will round out the whole into a full comprehension of the compounds, together with a tender care of other parts, will round out the whole of the compound of the inner, or circle of man's individual world; but a full comprehension of the compound into a perfect circle of man's physical and mental world, than is the exterior life. Objective life is the external circle of life. Dissatisfied one of nature or circle of objects sought. Man should live in his subjective realms and study before beginning a serious work; partial consultations, or God life, Consult with your inner life, than in real life. Dream life should be sought, when a true home counsel would have brought material advice only, often brings defeat of your whole life. Dream life is fuller of meaning and making beautiful more success and consequent happiness and making beautiful more, in his own world through, in his subjective realms and making beautiful more success and consequent happiness, often brings defeat of objects sought, when a true home counsel would have brought his relation to other compositions, or circles; thus fructifying and study intercourse with others who have worked in the great storehouse of subjectivity, and who have climbed already from the basement into the house of subjectivity, and who have climbed already from the basement into the great storehouse through, into the light or spiritual sunshine. To feed on material diet alone, contracts and distorts the circle of the man; but a full comprehension of the compounds should be avoided in real life. Man should live in his subjective realms, he enlarges or contracts throughout his own existence, and fitting into his place in the zone of creative life, if in the revolutions of the great circle he enlarges or contracts his own circle, a proper manna as it is the needs of the circle of life, in the great body of life.

date   thoughts
_____

_____

_____

_____
                                  emotions
_____

_____
                                  dream
_____

_____

_____

_____

_____

_____

_____
                         feelings upon awakening
_____

_____

_____
                                  comments
_____

_____

To dream of a ventriloquist, denotes that some treasonable affair is going to prove detrimental to your interest. If you think yourself one, you will not conduct yourself honorably towards people who trust you. For a young woman to dream she is mystified by the voice of ventriloquist, foretells that she will be deceived into illicit adventures.

‹Ventriloquist›

To dream that you are sending valentines, foretells that you will lose opportunities of enriching yourself.For a young woman to receive one, denotes that she will marry a weak, but ardent lover against the counsels of her guardians.

‹Valentine›

‹Violets›

To see violets in your dreams, or gather them, brings joyous occasions in which you will find favor with some superior person.For a young woman to gather them, denotes that she will soon meet her future husband.

‹Vine›

To dream of vines, is propitious of success and happiness.Good health is in store for those who see flowering vines.

To see a volcano in your dreams, signifies that you will be in violent disputes, which threaten your reputation as a fair dealing and honest citizen.For a young woman, it means that her selfishness and greed will lead her into intricate adventures.

‹Volcano›

To see, or hear a violin in dreams, foretells harmony and peace in the family, and financial affairs will cause no apprehension.For a young woman to play on one in her dreams, denotes that she will be honored and receive lavish gifts.

‹Violin›

date   thoughts

emotions

dream

feelings upon awakening

comments

Closely following in the wake of our multiplying evil thoughts are armies of these ghastly spectres pursuing each other with the exact intents and purposes of the mind that gave them being.

Thoughts are the subjective and creative force that produces action. Action is the objective effect of thought; hence the character of our daily thoughts is making our failure or success of to-morrow.

If we consider well these facts we will be forced into thinking our best thoughts at all times

date   thoughts
_____

_____

_____

_____

                        emotions
_____

_____

_____

                        dream
_____

_____

_____

_____

_____

_____

_____

_____

            feelings upon awakening
_____

_____

_____

                        comments
_____

_____

Plutarch relates how Augustus, while ill, through the dream of a friend, was persuaded to leave his tent, which a few hours after was captured by the enemy, and the bed whereon he had lain was pierced with the enemies' swords.

The prophets and those who have stood nearest the fountain of universal knowledge used dreams with more frequency than any other mode of divination.

Profane, as well as sacred, history is threaded with incidents of dream prophecy. Ancient history relates that Gennadius was convinced of the immortality of his soul by conversing with an apparition in his dream.

If Julius Caesar had been less incredulous about dreams he would have listened to the warning which Calpurnia, his wife, received in a dream.

Croesus saw his son killed in a dream.

Plato concurred in the general idea prevailing in his day, that there were divine manifestations to the soul in sleep. Condorcet thought and wrote with greater fluency in his dreams than in waking life.

Plato concurred in the general idea prevailing in his day, that there were divine manifestations to the soul in sleep. Condorcet thought and wrote with greater fluency in his dreams than in waking life.

The writers of Greek and Latin classics relate many instances of dream experiences. Homer accorded to some dreams divine origin. During the third and fourth centuries, the supernatural origin of dreams was so generally accepted that the fathers, relying upon the classics and the Bible as authority, made this belief a doctrine of the Christian Church.

Cicero relates the story of two traveling Arcadians who went to different lodgings—one to an inn, and the other to a private house. During the night the latter dreamed that his friend was begging for help. The dreamer awoke; but, thinking the matter unworthy of notice, went to sleep again. The second time he dreamed his friend appeared, saying it would be too late, for he had already been murdered and his body hid in a cart, under manure. The cart was afterward sought for and the body found. Cicero also wrote, ``If the gods love men they will certainly disclose their purposes to them in sleep."

Synesius placed dreaming above all methods of divining the future; he thought it the surest, and open to the poor and rich alike.

Aristotle wrote: ``There is a divination concerning some things in dreams not incredible." Camille Flammarion, in his great book on ``Premonitory Dreams and Divination of the Future," says: ``I do not hesitate to affirm at the outset that occurrence of dreams foretelling future events with accuracy must be accepted as certain."

Joan of Arc predicted her death.

date   thoughts

_____

_____

_____

                        emotions

_____

_____

                        dream

_____

_____

_____

_____

_____

_____

_____

                feelings upon awakening

_____

_____

                        comments

_____

A young woman, adored by her husband, dies at Moscow. Her father-in-law, at Pulkowo, near St. Petersburg, saw her that same hour by his side. She walked with him along the street; then she disappeared. Surprised, startled, and terrified, he telegraphed to his son, and learned both the sickness and the death of his daughter-in-law.

We are absolutely obliged to admit that SOMETHING emanated from the dying woman and touched her father-in-law. This thing unknown may have been an ethereal movement, as in the case of light, and may have been only an effect, a product, a result; but this effect must have had a cause, and this cause evidently proceeded from the woman who was dying. Can the constitution of the brain explain this projection? I do not think that any anatomist or physiologist will give this question an affirmative answer. One feels that there is a force unknown, proceeding, not from our physical organization, but from that in us which can think.

A lady in her own house hears a voice singing. It is the voice of a friend now in a convent, and she faints, because she is sure it is the voice of the dead. At the same moment that friend does really die, twenty miles away from her.

``The wife of a captain who has gone out to the Indian mutiny sees one night her husband standing before her with his hands pressed to his breast, and a look of suffering on his face. The agitation that she feels convinces her that he is either killed or badly wounded. It was November 14th. The War Office subsequently publishes his death as having taken place on November 15th. She endeavors to have the true date ascertained. The War Office was wrong. He died on the 14th.

A child six years old stops in the middle of his play and cries out, frightened: Mamma, I have seen Mamma." At that moment his mother was dying far away from him

A young girl at a ball stops short in the middle of a dance and cries, bursting into tears. `My father is dead; I have just seen him.' At that moment her father died. She did not even know he was ill.

date   thoughts
_____

_____

_____

_____

                        emotions

_____

_____

                        dream

_____

_____

_____

_____

_____

_____

_____

_____

                  feelings upon awakening

_____

_____

_____

                        comments

_____

All these things present themselves to us as indicating not physiological operations of one brain acting on another, but psychic actions of spirit upon spirit. We feel that they indicate to us some power unknown.

No doubt it is difficult to apportion what belongs to the spirit, the soul, and what belongs to the brain. We can only let ourselves be guided in our judgment and our appreciations by the same feeling that is created
in us by the discussion of phenomena. This is how all science has been started.

*Well, and does not every
one feel that we have here to do with manifestations
from beings capable of thought, and not with
material physiological facts only?*

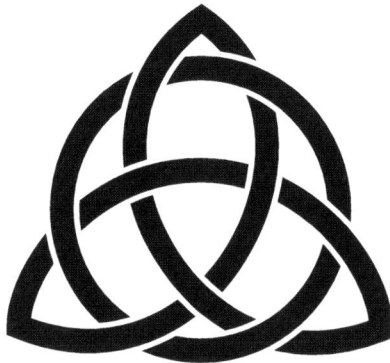

date   thoughts

_____

_____

_____

                        emotions

_____

_____

                        dream

_____

_____

_____

_____

_____

_____

_____

                  feelings upon awakening

_____

_____

_____

                        comments

_____

1. Man is the microcosm or a miniature world. He has a soul and mental firmament, bounded by the stellar dust and the milky way, and filled with the mystery of suns, satellites and stars. These he can study best by the astronomy of induction and introspection.

2. He has also a physical plane, diversified by oceans, lakes, rivers, fertile valleys, waste places and mountains. All are in cosmic interdependency as they are in the macrocosm. Here rests the mystery of being—the new grandest phenomena of subjects!

3. The student is no less bewildered and awed than the geologist who gropes blindly through the seams of the earth searching for links in the infinite chain of knowledge, or the astronomer sweeping the heavens.

4. The two planes are dependent upon each other. It is the smile or disease of the firmament that blesses or diseases the earth. It is likewise the impure firmament of the microcosm that diseases the body and soul.

5. If it reflects the drought of thought or the various states of evil, deserts will enlarge, forest of infectious, venomous growth will form the habitation of lust and murder.

6. Before great moral or physical revolutions or catastrophes occur, clouds will darken the horizon of the dream mind; storms will gather, lurid flames of lightning will flash their volatile anger; the explosive thunder will recklessly carry on its bombardment; bells will ring, strange knocking will be heard—symbols of a message— phantom forms will be seen, familiar voices will call and plead with you, unknown visitors will threaten you, unearthly struggles with hideous giants and agonies of mind and body will possess you; malformations of the most hideous type will seize your vision; shrouded in sheets of a whitish vapor, evanescent specters, with pallid face and of warning countenance, will cling around you, and contagion and famine will leave their desolate impress upon the flower of health and in the field of plenty.

7. Thus all of us would be nightly warned in our circle or miniature world if we would develop subjective strength to retain the impressions left upon our dream mind

8. But in spite of all reason and conscience— in spite of the inductive knowledge received through our senses— we go on from day to day, and step by step, feeding our soul on the luscious fruit of the outward senses, until the rank weeds of selfishness(sic) have choked out all other forces.

9. Thus the soul is filled with thought images that assume the form of vicious animals, homely visaged fowls, rabid and snarling cats and dogs, leprous and virile serpents, cankerous lizards, slimy intestine worms, hairy and malicious insects. They are generated by greed, envy, jealousy, covetousness, backbiting, amorous longings and other impure thoughts.

10. With the soul filled with this conglomeration of virus and filth, why doubt a hell and its counterpart condition, or expect the day or night to bring happiness? If evil thoughts will infest the soul with ravenous microbes, good thoughts and deeds will starve and suppress their activity, and create a heaven to supplant them.

11. With this grand and eternal truth in view, man should ever think kindly of those about him, control his temper in word and action, seek his own, think the best of thoughts, study to relieve the worthy poor, seek solace in the depth of being, and let gentleness and meekness characterize his life. Then will he sow the seeds of a present and future heaven.

13. His day thoughts and his night thoughts in harmony will point with unerring forecast to a peaceful end. Spiritual and helpful warnings will fall upon the dream mind, as gently as dew upon the flowers and as softly as a mother's kiss upon the lips of love.

14. When our external lives are guided by the forces within, sweet are the words and messages from our own spirit; for those who are truly blessed are those who seek divine love through the channels of their inner world of consciousness.

A DIAGRAM GIVING THE THEORY OF THIS BOOK, AND THE RELATIONSHIP BETWEEN THE MICROCOSM AND THE MACROCOSM.

date   thoughts

_____

_____

_____

                                  emotions

_____

_____

                                  dream

_____

_____

_____

_____

_____

_____

_____

                        feelings upon awakening

_____

_____

                                  comments

_____

Wager To dream of making a wager, signifies that you will resort to dishonest means to forward your schemes. If you lose a wager, you will sustain injury from base connections with those out of your social sphere. To win one, reinstates you in favor with fortune.

Walnut To dream of walnuts, is an omen significant of prolific joys and favors.

Washboard To see a washboard in your dreams, is indicative of embarrassment. If you see a woman using one, it predicts that you will let women rob you of energy and fortune. A broken one, portends that you will come to grief and disgraceful deeds through fast living.

Walking Stick To see a walking stick in a dream, foretells you will enter into contracts without proper deliberation, and will consequently suffer reverses. If you use one in walking, you will be dependent upon the advice of others. To admire handsome ones, you will entrust your interest to others, but they will be faithful.

War To dream of war, foretells unfortunate conditions in business, and much disorder and strife in domestic affairs. For a young woman to dream that her lover goes to war, denotes that she will hear of something detrimental to her lover's character.

Whirlwind To dream that you are in the path of a whirlwind, foretells that you are confronting a change which threatens to overwhelm you with loss and calamity.

Waltz To see the waltz danced, foretells that you will have pleasant relations with a cheerful and adventuresome person.

Whistle To hear a whistle in your dream, denotes that you will be shocked by some sad intelligence, which will change your plans laid for innocent pleasure.

date   thoughts

_____

_____

_____

_____

                        emotions

_____

_____

_____

                        dream

_____

_____

_____

_____

_____

_____

_____

_____

                 feelings upon awakening

_____

_____

_____

                        comments

_____

_____

This impression is superabundantly confirmed by investigation concerning the unknown faculties of the soul, when active in dreams and somnambulism.

- A brother learns the death of his young sister by a terrible nightmare.
- A young girl sees beforehand, in a dream, the man whom she will marry.
- A mother sees her child lying in a road, covered with blood.
- A lady goes, in a dream, to visit her husband on a distant steamer, and her husband really receives this visit, which is seen by a third person.
- A gentleman sees, in a dream, a lady whom he knows arriving at night in a railroad station, her journey having been undertaken suddenly.
- A magistrate sees three years in advance the commission of a crime, down to its smallest details.
- Several persons report that they have seen towns and landscapes before they ever visited them, and have seen themselves in situations in which they found themselves long after.
- A mother hears her daughter announce her intended marriage six months before it has been thought of.
- Frequent cases of death are foretold with precision.
- A theft is seen by a somnambulist, and the execution of the criminal is foretold.
- A young girl sees her fiance', or an intimate friend dying (these are frequent cases), etc.

All these show unknown faculties in the soul. It seems to me that we cannot reasonably attribute the prevision of the future and mental sight to a nervous action of the brain." I think we must either deny these facts or admit that they must have had an intellectual and spiritual cause of the psychic order, and I recommend sceptics who do not desire to be convinced, to deny them outright; to treat them as illusions and cases of a fortuitous coincidence of circumstances. They will find this easier. Uncompromising deniers of facts, rebels against evidence, may be all the more positive, and may declare that the writers of these extraordinary narratives are persons fond of a joke, who have written them to hoax me; and that there have been persons in all ages who have done the same thing to mystify thinkers who have taken up such questions.

date   thoughts

_____

_____

_____

_____

                                  emotions

_____

_____

                                  dream

_____

_____

_____

_____

_____

_____

_____

_____

                       feelings upon awakening

_____

_____

_____

                                  comments

_____

These phenomena prove, *I think,* **that the soul exists,** *and that it is endowed with faculties at present unknown.*

date   thoughts

emotions

dream

feelings upon awakening

comments

That is the logical way of commencing our study, which in the end may lead us to the problem of the after-life and immortality. A thought can be transmitted to the mind of another. There are mental transmissions, communications of thoughts, and psychic currents between human souls. It is optional with man to obtain spiritual or material supply to some of the needs of the circle, a proper denial of material diet alone, will round out the whole into a perfect circle of life. Dissentious and conflicting results should be avoided in computing the length and breadth of the compounds, together with a tender care of other parts, the mind receives education from communing with the dream composition in the great circle. Consult with your whole nature or circle before beginning a serious work; partial consultations, or material advice only, often brings defeat of objects sought, when a true home or circle would have brought success and consequent happiness. Man should live in his subjective realms and study more his relation to other compositions or circles, and who have climbed already from the basement, through intercourse with others who have worked in the great storehouse of subjectivity, fructifying and making beautiful the light of spiritual sunshine. Objective life is one of the smallest compounds in real life. Dream life is fuller of meaning and teaching in the inner, or God life, than is the exterior life of man, the individual world.

Space appears to be no obstacle in these cases, and time sometimes seems to be

ANNIHILATED

date   thoughts

emotions

dream

feelings upon awakening

comments

The sleeping mind is not only supersensitive as to existing external sounds and light, but it frequently sees hours and days ahead of the waking mind.

In sleep we see, without being awakened, the angry lightning rend the midnight clouds, and hear the explosive thunder hurl its fury at us; but can we explain it any more than our scientist can explain the natural forces of thought, of love and hate, or the subtle intuition of woman?

date _____ thoughts _____

_____

_____

_____

emotions

_____

_____

dream

_____

_____

_____

_____

_____

_____

_____

feelings upon awakening

_____

_____

comments

_____

Yard Stick To dream of a yard stick, foretells much anxiety will possess you, though your affairs assume unusual activity. Yarn.

Yarn To dream of yarn, denotes success in your business and an industrious companion in your home. For a young woman to dream that she works with yarn, foretells that she will be proudly recognized by a worthy man as his wife.

Yoke To dream of seeing a yoke, denotes that you will unwillingly conform to the customs and wishes of others. To yoke oxen signifies that your judgment will be accepted submissively by those dependent upon you.

Y

Yacht To see a yacht in a dream, denotes happy recreation away from business and troublesome encumbrances. A stranded one, represents miscarriage of entertaining engagements.

Yield To dream you yield to another's wishes, denotes that you will throw away by weak indecision a great opportunity to elevate yourself. If others yield to you, exclusive privileges will be accorded you and you will be elevated above your associates. To receive poor yield for your labors, you may expect cares and worries.

Young To dream of seeing young people, is a prognostication of reconciliation of family disagreements and favorable times for planning new enterprises.

date   thoughts

_____

_____

_____

                                  emotions

_____

_____

                                   dream

_____

_____

_____

_____

_____

_____

_____

                        feelings upon awakening

_____

_____

                                  comments

_____

The house vacated by the selfish appetites of the world would be filled with the whispers of spiritual love and wisdom necessary to the mutual welfare and development of body and soul.

date

thoughts

_____

_____

_____

emotions

_____

_____

dream

_____

_____

_____

_____

_____

_____

_____

feelings upon awakening

_____

_____

comments

_____

Thoughts proceed from the visible mind and dreams from the invisible mind. The average waking mind receives and retains only a few of the lessons of life. It is largely filled with idle and incoherent thoughts that are soon forgotten. The same may be truly said of the dream mind. Many of our day thoughts are day dreams, just as many of our night dreams are night thoughts. Our day deeds of evil or good pierce or soothe the conscience, just as our night symbols of sorrow and joy sadden or please the objective senses. Our day's thoughts are filled with the warnings and presence of the inner mind and our night's thoughts are tinctured and often controlled by our external mind.

date   thoughts

_____

_____

_____

                                  emotions

_____

_____

                                   dream

_____

_____

_____

_____

_____

_____

_____

                        feelings upon awakening

_____

_____

_____

                                 comments

_____

_____

A FEW QUESTIONS AND

ANSWERS

REGARDING DREAMS.

What

is a dream?

A dream is an event transpiring in that world belonging to the mind when the objective senses have withdrawn into rest or oblivion.

Then the spiritual man is living alone in the future or ahead of objective life and consequently lives man's future first, developing conditions in a way that enables waking man to shape his actions by warnings, so as to make life a perfect existence.

date   thoughts

_____

_____

_____

                              emotions

_____

_____

                               dream

_____

_____

_____

_____

_____

_____

                    feelings upon awakening

_____

_____

                             comments

_____

A woman may see a serpent in waking life and through fright lose reason or self-control. She imagines it pursues her when in reality it is going an opposite direction; in a like way dreams may be many times unreal.

Now, the woman's face was only the expression of her real thoughts and the state of her business combined. Her thoughts were strong and healthy, but her business flagging, hence her own spirit is not a perfect likeness of her own soul, as it takes every atom of earthly composition perfectly normal to reproduce a perfect spirit picture of the soul or mortal woman. She would have seen a true likeness of herself had conditions been favorable; thus a woman knows when a complete whole is her portion.

Study to make surroundings always harmonious.

Life is only being perfectly carried on when these conditions are in unison.

date   thoughts

_____

_____

_____

                        emotions

_____

_____

                         dream

_____

_____

_____

_____

_____

_____

                 feelings upon awakening

_____

_____

                        comments

_____

ZENITH TO DREAM OF THE ZENITH, FORETELLS ELABORATE PROSPERITY, AND YOUR CHOICE OF SUITORS WILL BE SUCCESSFUL.

ZEBRA TO DREAM OF A ZEBRA, DENOTES THAT YOU WILL BE INTERESTED IN VARYING AND FLEETING ENTERPRISES.TO SEE ONE WILD IN HIS NATIVE COUNTRY, FORETELLS THAT YOU WILL PURSUE A CHIMERICAL FANCY WHICH WILL RETURN YOU UNSATISFACTORY PLEASURE UPON POSSESSION.

ZEPHYR TO DREAM OF SOFT ZEPHYRS, DENOTES THAT YOU WILL SACRIFICE FORTUNE TO OBTAIN THE OBJECT OF YOUR AFFECTION AND WILL FIND RECIPROCAL AFFECTION IN YOUR WOOING.IF A YOUNG WOMAN DREAMS THAT SHE IS SADDENED BY THE WHISPERINGS OF THE ZEPHYRS, SHE WILL HAVE A SEASON OF DISQUIETUDE BY THE COMPELLED ABSENCE OF HER LOVER.

ZINC TO WORK WITH OR TO SEE ZINC IN YOUR DREAMS, INDICATES SUBSTANTIAL AND ENERGETIC PROGRESS. BUSINESS WILL ASSUME A BRISK TONE IN ITS VARYING DEPARTMENTS.TO DREAM OF ZINC ORE PROMISES THE APPROACH OF EVENTFUL SUCCESS.

ZODIAC TO DREAM OF THE ZODIAC IS A PROGNOSTICATION OF UNPARALLELED RISE IN MATERIAL WORTH, BUT ALSO INDICATES ALLOYED PEACE AND HAPPINESS.TO SEE IT APPEARING WEIRD, DENOTES THAT SOME UNTOWARD GRIEF IS HOVERING OVER YOU AND IT WILL TAKE STRENUOUS EFFORTS TO DISPEL IT.TO STUDY THE ZODIAC IN YOUR DREAMS,

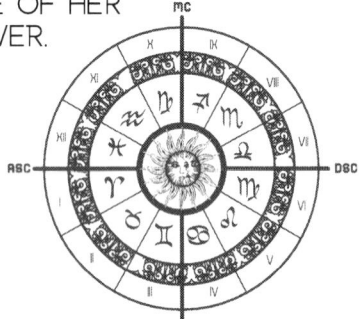

IT ALSO DENOTES THAT YOU WILL GAIN DISTINCTION AND FAVOR BY YOUR INTERCOURSE WITH STRANGERS.IF YOU APPROACH IT OR IT APPROACHES YOU, FORETELLS THAT YOU WILL SUCCEED IN YOUR SPECULATIONS TO THE WONDERMENT OF OTHERS AND BEYOND YOUR WILDEST IMAGINATION.TO DRAW A MAP OF IT, SIGNIFIES FUTURE GAIN.

date   thoughts

_____

_____

_____

_____

emotions

_____

_____

_____

dream

_____

_____

_____

_____

_____

_____

_____

_____

feelings upon awakening

_____

_____

_____

comments

_____

_____

Q.—What Relationship is sustained between the average man and his dreams?

A.—A dream to the average or sensual person, bears the same Relation to his objective life that it maintained in the case of the ideal dreamer, but it means pleasures, sufferings and advancements on a lower or material plane.

Q.—If that is so, why can't you tell us accurately of our future as you do of our past?

A.—Because events are like a procession; they pass a few at a time and cast a shadow on subjective minds, and those which have passed before the waking mind are felt by other minds also and necessarily make a more lasting impression on the subjective mind.

Q.—Then why is man not always able to correctly interpret his dreams?

A.—Just as words fail sometimes to express ideas, so dreams fail sometimes in their mind pictures to portray coming events.

Q.—How does subjectivity deal with time?

A.—There is no past and future to subjectivity. It is all one living present.

Q.—If they relate to the future, why is it we so often dream of the past?

A.—When a person dreams of the present, past events, those events are warnings of evil or good; sometimes they are stamped so indelibly upon the subjective mind that the least tendency of the waking mind to the past throws these pictures in relief on the dream consciousness.

Q.—Why is it that present environments often influence our dreams?

A.—Because the future of man is usually affected by the present, so if he mars the present by wilful wrongs, or makes it bright by right living it will necessarily have influence on his dreams, as they are forecastings of the future.

Q.—To illustrate: A person retiring or closing his eyes had a face appear to him, the forehead well formed but the lower parts distorted. Explain this phenomenon?

A.—A change of state from perfect sleep or waking possessed him.

Q.—WHAT IS AN APPARITION?

A.—IT IS THE SUBJECTIVE MIND STORED WITH THE WISDOM GAINED FROM FUTURITY, AND IN ITS STRENUOUS EFFORTS TO WARN ITS PRESENT HABITATION—THE CORPORAL BODY—OF DANGERS JUST AHEAD, TAKES ON THE SHAPE OF A DEAR ONE AS THE MOST EFFECTIVE METHOD OF IMPARTING THIS KNOWLEDGE.

date   thoughts

_____

_____

_____

emotions

_____

_____

dream

_____

_____

_____

_____

_____

_____

feelings upon awakening

_____

_____

comments

_____

_____

Made in the USA
Las Vegas, NV
28 July 2021